zombie love

zombie love

j k lawson

First published in the USA in 2021 by
White Lane Press, Plymouth, United Kingdom.

ISBN 978-0-9568488-7-1

John K. Lawson is a visual artist and poet. His work can be found in many private and public collections both in the USA and UK. His three most recent books *Juke Joint Men, Maker Rebirth* and *Figures in Jazz* combine his poetry and visual art in provocative dialogue with each other. His poetry is regularly published in The Berkshire Edge and Country Roads in the USA.

By the same author

Juke Joint Men
Maker Rebirth
Figures in Jazz
Hurricane Hotel
Now
A Map of Sorts

Acknowledgements

I am grateful to everyone who encouraged this poetic journey, from my humble beginnings many moons ago in Westwords, to The Berkshire Edge and Country Roads.

I thank Dr James Zachary and Nick Keene for their visual contributions, my editor Mark Penwill at White Lane Press, fellow wandering bard John Kearns for his honest foreword and you, the reader, for inspiring this trilogy into fruition and to whom this collection is dedicated.

Several of these poems first appeared in The Berkshire Edge, Country Roads and Juke Joint Men.

Front cover image: *Zombie Love* by J K Lawson, 2018.
Salvaged flood damaged drawings, collage and paint. 48 x 36 cm.
Collection of Dr Jim Zachary.

Contents

Foreword

It is my pleasure and privilege to introduce, the third and final work in his series of books for White Lane Press, Zombie Love, by John K. Lawson, my fellow sojourner in the poetic life.

John K. Lawson lives, creates, promotes and shares as a true poet and artist. He not only travels but explores and observes. In his art and poetry, he portrays people, places, experiences, and tragedies as well as the hope that springs from them.

I, too, am an artist of more than one discipline, a writer of fiction, plays, poems as well as a songwriter and guitar player. I have published the short-story collection, Dreams and Dull Realities and the novel, The World, and my new novel, Worlds. I have had plays produced in New York and in Dublin. Many of my poems have been published in literary journals.

For seven years, I produced the Irish-American Writers and Artists (IAW&A) Salons, a volunteer-run series which gives established, emerging, and beginning artists brief slots in which to present their work — for free and for equal attention from the audience. JK shared his work with the IAW&A audience one memorable night in 2019.

I first encountered JK when I was invited to read poetry with him in a narrow, white-walled gallery in Manhattan's Chelsea district. His beautiful and haunting Mardi-Gras-beaded piano Temptation eyeballed me and the entire gathering throughout the event.

The second time our paths crossed we were both featured readers at the Saturn Series at the Shades of Green pub in New York's Grammercy section. JK read his poetry along with the music of Mark Tuomenoksa and Sarah Kohrs. We poets in the back room struggled to be heard over the jukebox that no one would turn down in the front room. My indelible memory of that night was JK's riding off with Temptation on the back of a pickup truck along the cramped streets near Irving Place shouting vague arrangements for the next adventure.

The next adventure was JK's joining us at the IAW&A Salon. This time he created spontaneous poetry bop, reading his work along with the music of saxophone maestro Jon Gordon whose horn mimicked the thrumming of a helicopter as it searched New Orleans rooftops for Katrina survivors.

Afterwards, we feasted on Guinness and mussels at a nearby dive, staying long after I should have been home in my have-to-get-up-for-work-in-the-morning bed. We were a group of artists eating and drinking and connecting. We searched for the last mussels in the bottoms of bowls murky with white-wine-garlic sauce the way we search for beauty. The next morning JK even connected over a cup of coffee with my Chinese mother in-law who speaks no English.

Our most recent encounter occurred as the pandemic was easing in May 2021. JK introduced me to writer and singer April Lee Fields who graciously allowed me to join her show at The Pearl Lounge in the Bywater section of New Orleans. It was my first performance in 17 months, my first ever in New Orleans, and the first in-person promotion for my new novel, Worlds.

My wife and I were on a work-from-home tour of the South, high-fiving dead writers and musicians along the way: Thomas Wolfe and Howlin' Wolf, The King and BB King, and William Faulkner and Flannery O'Connor. I arrived at The Pearl in a cowboy hat bought near Ryman Auditorium in Nashville, a shirt from Sun Studios in Memphis, and a shell casing from Jerry Lee Lewis's ranch in my guitar case.

To gain entrance to the Pearl on Desire Street, you knock on the high rough-hewn fence. You are welcomed to the speakeasy of challenging spoken word. The ground feels unsteady underfoot before you finish your first beer. But soon you are chatting by a bathtub full of oyster shells with a flames dancing in a firepit behind you, as darkness and the crowd arrives for the outdoor performance. A backyard spaceship welcomes several passengers and the words, the singing, the slithering bass, and the solid jazzdrums blast you to the crescent moon above Bywater. By the continent-dividing, crescent-shaped Mississippi water, that is.

JK and I have had fun evenings, certainly, but there are struggles along with the laughs. We both toil to produce artistic work in a society that doesn't make that easy. My books have been published by small presses, and I need to promote them myself. I have had to produce my own plays in Manhattan which requires expense and time after a full workday — a hectic schedule of rehearsing, running around in search of props like easels, school desks, or salads. My IAW&A Salon work included fetching beer and wine, collecting donations, paying bills, and working with venue-owners with Manhattan bottom-line rather than artistic concerns.

John does the same with his art and poetry — collecting beads in New Orleans, driving his Mardi-Gras pianos to distant galleries, collaborating with and encouraging other artists, living the pikey poet life from to Baton Rouge to the Berkshires to Cornwall. He does the same with his limited-edition books of poetry and art like Zombie Love.

Yet we undertake and persist in these struggles. We toss our stones from the Bywater and hope the ripples spread across rivers and oceans.

Because we are poets in the ancient Greek sense, people who ποιεν (poien) make.

Because we are called to this work despite societal demands or indifference.
Because the work must be done. There is no other choice.
Because the work must be shared. There is no other way.

You have knocked on the door. Now enter the adventure of Zombie Love.

John Kearns
Nashville — Savannah — New York
May 2021

zombie love

-germ warfare starts with a sneeze-

zombie love

spectral splendor
mists seeping serene

the birth of today lives on
muddy boots and ankles

laces walk waist high in ghosts
this kernow mist shares

our open road home unopened
ketchup packs refrigerate themselves

crisscrossed nights surpassed surprises
jean zippers burst

wildness inspired children
going up with flames

half eaten alive returning
to this our oceans pledge

sparkling light
cascading giggles

two cokes in a can

conceived in diets of trust
howling with madness prescribed

reduced now to finally
off all that crap

in rusted zoom lenses
we submerge

dusted
cobwebbed

between doctored rooms
pyche wards and lock downs

flying high five knowing
the crime of moderation
rarely acts nice

fingerprints

this full blown scream depicts
Sisyphus pushing a pipeline across plains
past pristine forests scared in sacred lands
humble back yards backing extinction
as landscapes blur bitter in rain
images beckon with scribbled eyes on
an 80 year sprung lady
enthroned in native head dress
handcuffed to a wheel chair
and escorted away with logic
derived from a loaded gun

concealed under bed covers
children weep in nursery rhymes
why bother with commitment
when all that matters is this moment
tagged with gum under chairs
some say we venture on
lost in misplaced vacuums
desire caught continually off guard
in a web ushering daylight
rebirth candles melt
after being up all night doing what
naked people do best

meanwhile
back in her last forty
a few brave souls dress in raincoats
before boarding unlocked schools buses
a slog for sure churning into this Otis mist
whispering can we share a coffee cup
numbed out by a law of averages

yes perhaps
in the laugh before the first refill
he or she you or me
without fingerprints enticing the touch pad
can delete outdated messages
long ago scribbled in sand

yes perhaps
without fingerprints
can we accept we are products
of man/women/child/ you me them
clicking through me phone
to like children with torn mittens hurling Pepsi cans
at armed police cars covered in a glowing green snow
fallen on a hot sunny day
to fight or fend off
squeezed clean dreams
stubborn enough to knuckle down
and press repeat

meanwhile
back in her lost forty
answers from fallen angels deranged as poets
depict amputated success failing
as fake news broadcasts faceless facts
with no hint of ending clean cut lies
revealed on razor barb wire fences
littered with posters advertising five dollar hair cuts
with luck gold teeth replacements
and one eight hundred numbers offering to buy up
poisoned lots scorched in lost dreams
while two overworked under paid cops
drive away sirens blazing

the handcuffed grandma booked as a pipeline
slouches through Sandisfield
and once upon a time history
mangles with destiny

blunt needles

we fidget as usual
scribbling down coughed out words
blank prescriptions thrown in between fly by angels
fleeing one more no name heaven
curled in disbelief
masks and plastic gloved hands represent
the invisible strength of science
strong enough
to shake or break this glass reflecting panic
inside this make shift clinic
housed alongside a besieged Walmart

i admit she says
to the guy nodding off beside me

all this waiting in line
for a test or the next wannabe cure
leads me to believe i have witnessed enough fake news
to acknowledge how those grey haired creepy geezers
resemble you now rambling on for hours weeks and months
always complaining in the last gasp
how we should have done this
or how we should never have done that

in fact to be poetic you are like a squishy fart
or worse pigeon shit on my freshly washed camper
a faint drizzle cursed with boredom
until reeling off the seams
i throw you out only to have you
instantly magically reappear
a demented stained rabbit
jack hammering me phone
with whatever i guess i really never
ever want to know these daze

really he says
cleaning his nails with a safety pin
half breathing against my shoulder

you try being me cast back into
dismal depths of domesticity
at least i admit zero need to pay any bills on time
at least after selling blood then plasma all day
i get to count echoes bouncing on every Chet Baker beat

bobbing across the universe ear to ear
have you ever really listened to Snoop Dog

his mirrored memories transcend
always a stone throw away
half resembling a borrowed Satchmo trumpet
or my peddled headphones
pawned like one of your pops rare coins
later found as a fake on a dance floor
before a bunch of machetes
beat the crap out of us

you remember that night
oh please tell me you do

of course i do silly she smiles at her phone
pushing his carcass towards me sniffing
why do you always change the subject
somehow you make far more sense
when you simply shut up

long after your actions wear themselves out
with or without another one of your sagas

hinged on after all this time together
our relationship boils down to a blunt needle
in search of a fresh vein

silence ensues as i salvage a light
and remark with a sharpie the blood
on his bruised knuckles matches
her smashed up face

numbers are called perhaps to reassure
we are all the young undone

silence ensues before she screams fuck it
and they exit hand in hand with a little luck forgetting
the very reason why we ever assembled here
in the first place

who can wear a mask

who can wear a mask
when hugs and kisses weaponized death

after slugging all day tied to grinding engines
maniacal bulldozer claws

slabs broken for peanuts
over stressed and under paid

with a backo or without
me jack hammer

who can wear a mask
on factory stone lines as flinched faces stare thru

taped windows smeared in greased time
a reflection packing boxes for amazon

the free worldz answer to
assortment of free will

press pay now for yet more thousands
stuff doubled deep in debt stuff

who can wear a mask
with jumping tongues wagging

starvation equals salvation
numbed out and panic stricken

a lawyer tells me how a three job work load
per week

equates to common practice
for most of the many

who can wear a mask
drunk on unfiltered tap water unfit for dead flowers

pasted in condemned mission rooms
old souls mingle with children

shuffle lost bare feet
blistered beyond greed revealing

ever widening jaws and countless bloody wounds
manufactured without blame inner strange land

a map reveals all roads
lead to china

simple plan

there be a simple plan
huddled on board this sinking ferry

silenced as stale cereal spills on
unwashed dishes mounting

a forgetfulness to floss reminisces
a resurrection of holes

stuffed at the seams with crumpled masks
and faceless what nots

there be a simple plan
attributed to broken tastes

spinning with chipped plates
surrounded by useless trinkets

permanent grease stains
caged in wallpaper bird reminders

consumed by painting butterflies
plagued by dreams

with or without minutes spared

this is a simple plan
congested as odd ball thoughts arrive

first thing every damp morning
no need for prayer tormented in zit ridden youth

flecked with images on a phone
jokes resemble rusty nails

dressed hell bent scrounging for bus fair
in this our own home lock down town

there be a simple plan
swiped through living ghosts

armed with shovels
and make shift borrowed spades

ready to dig up wings circling
caked mud weighing on our boots as

slim chances reveal a last buck to shave
before tracking down my sister

to wipe the smirk of your face
and bury these bastards forever

ebb an flow

and so it goes
tabby thomas is wailing
hey bartender

ebb an flow
ebb an flow

for almost a month now dancing
tiny tim resembles a headless chicken
his body and the music inseparable

against all odds
folks seem to be behaving super nice
hogan and kelly are breaking chords with fire
scattered across folding tables half pints of whiskey
salted peanuts mingle with shuffled cards
cutting up beyond anything he needs to know

ebb n flow
ebb n flow

when closing time arrives
in the parking lot there is a shout and scuffle
tabby is chasing tiny tim with what looks like
a gun in his belt

you goin nowhere fast tonight shouts tabby
pointing at tiny timz truck
why not tiny tim pleads
because it is painted black and white
like a one of them dairy holstein cows
that is why bellows tabby

i remain proud of that fact
tiny tim beams leaning on the tailgate
before sliding like melting ice
onto the tarmac floor

listen up tabby inhales
i am not joking or taking any crap
you are as crazy as you dance
not my problem however this time at night
there is a man at one end of this here one way street
and another waiting at the other end
trust me you will never get past either of them
in a truck painted like a dairy cow

what do i do asks tiny tim
already crashing in the back of his truck

ebb an flow
son
ebb an flow

coffee mixes

our ceiling fan stopped spinning
earlier lightening replaced electricity

and in these hours after black outs
this storm joins our skin like a fresh open wound

coffee mixes with chicory making
the impossible seem a little more possible again

tempting us to think if we keep our masks on
we can step outside and reach for a higher state

however inadequate a flooded home sounds
letz do it you say take a walk find a park

with a swing and a pond
roll around naked in the dark

can we descend now you dance mirrored
to this my unhinged image

like a forgotten misplaced letter
stuffed in an no name locker

mesmerized by a plastic bag swirling through thick air
before settling beside your drenched boot prints

we claim tonight we are all of this world
humbled as if sent from the stars

the moon dances reflecting depths
a reminder perhaps to memorize

fallen tears offer little shelter

outside the dispensary

herded in line
freezing outside the dispensary
masked rain reflects boots brave enough
to walk on water mumbling we gather here
dumbed thumbs stuck in gaping mouths
gawking at disparity and failed austerity
filling dispensed trodden streets
from one side of a squeaky aisle
to the automatic disconnected next

dispensing dispensable things
all across this dispensable town
dispensing dispensable lives
with indispensable hope churned
out of dispensable preachers
mirrored as indispensable politicians
swearing upon indispensable oaths
indispensably make dispensable trillion
billions on dispensable backs of the dispensable
poor claiming wholesome indispensable
righteous commerce equates to dispensable
voters sold on indispensable happiness
with three jobs in this dispensable
heartland rusting to full stops
and worn thin blaming anyone who
happens to be dispensable dead enough
to dependably lie hard enough to think
indispensability has a shot at dispensable
redemption through unregulated greed
to stop resenting our dispensable parents
who knew no better yet somehow managed
dispensable indispensability to make
life happen with a whole lot less disposable
thumb sucking before we walk in

and purchase dispensable dreams
before walking out feeling
indispensably fine

papa and a rope

papa and a rope
tied to his waist

baptizes my soul in this
mighty spring fast flowing Mississippi

a staircase of rapid ripples
smashed with whiteness shivers

a choir of potential evolution
joins the endless power of beauty passing through

a gift wrapped with unborn song
washing over us

yeah your right wails a corn liquored preacher
from the safety of the receding levee

in the knowledge of becoming a tribe
undescribed emotions unites clarity

columns of matter built and broken
reflects trust in raw humility

this river pulses on past any given lock gates
like a decision recognized rejects open wounds

destined to unfold yesterdaze sounds float resurfacing
from depths yet to be fathomed or blessed

close by through cypress trees and knees
a heron swoops and the river replies

son no matter what
you choose to do

from this moment forth remember
the mosquito always bites

anonymous concrete

touch i say
touch and go listen to the empty tin can rattle
smudge wedding confetti washed against the curb
smudge the ruffled coats pinned to the ground
laced in booze and talking to themselves
with bitch ass sharpies

hear the wind whip yester daze news
mingled in alternative facts
mangled all the way to fake

hear the streets choke with beginners luck
fear printed in digital papers believing
passengers move with hidden cargos
strapped on a sleeve or photo shopped to receive
what is built to survive requires religion and walls
before another bombed out child
dies before ever being conceived

hear the click clicking heels of the bankers play thing
watch a gold chain grip on his limp wet wrist
wind up wind down
pull away the chords and let blinds fly
as fake austerity sets in
with frozen eyes blinking in reptilian greed

hear the deaf groan for living sounds
dangling on a buckle in remote control
dangling in a world on pendulum clocks
tick tock tock tick
half past ready to drop
with ever approaching speed

hear the rush of honored grown men vomit
sick from lack of welfare and unpayable fees
there seems to be oh so much and yet oh so little time
to send us all back to who knows where

touch i say
touch and go listen as young boys and girls
leave their chalk rooms
dressed up skirts about to be stained on grass
in the locker or behind the proverbial bike shed

again the question of importance
before mother arrives
tightly dressed in an older version
yet far less tamed
mimicking mindless adverts
and the bankers play thing

and fashion changes fashion beats
the chance to enslave foreign rag dolls
to bend and stretch around tattooed cocks
ringed in vice with a royal flush
a slave trade without borders
oh yes fashion changes fashion beats

touch i say
touch and go listen
to a flag rope hitting the flag pole
no flag is in sight and yet we all wave
perhaps it has been stolen or missing in action
no flag is in sight and yet we all wave

here shop windows are no longer dressed
to rumors of bargained for much needed goods
offering false promises to a promised child
whose broken lips press against this
shattered glass

here again on a bench in the park
derelict men pipe over old print
reminiscing oh to be youthful they wheeze
unable to acknowledge germ warfare
starts with a sneeze

here a hotel room is no safer than my pockets
here i can taste salt on pickled fish eyes
here i have the time to fry in snow
as collars are tightened around sore throats

here again no time to question
manicured fists punching out mechanized time
for the very last time
before anonymous concrete
spews onto cracked streets
buckled with question mark grimaces
as statues fall and anchors let go
masked breathing muffles
bring it on mother fuckers
this is amerikkka

chewing gum

think about real poets she types
anyone who can take it for so long
perfectly disjointed offers a chance to be remembered
even now as you need so much for me to say
and yet rarely really listen
i like the titles of your poems the best

absently focusing on the drizzle securing our progress
she continues your themes however are too easy
they lack momentum or any kind of drive
trying to cram mistakes into gooey globs of insightfulness
the end results alas an endless mess
sticky semi hard ooze
kinda like chewing gum

chewing gum
he blurts questioning perched on the porch
busted in the realization these daze he uses a pocket knife
when eating marmite on toast

yes chewing gum you know
kinda like the kind underneath this excuse for a kitchen table
sticking to my fingers and this
my new recycled marks and sparks floral dress

our eyes

these eyes
watch a mother crying
in a twice weekly plasma bag
feeding her hungry children
lost on side warped streets

your eyes
hear the homeless sigh
with their bleached lips licking
household bottled cleaning brands
domestic ulcers threw away

my eyes
spat on bullies
wearing righteous neckties
kicking a hungry shoplifter
behind day-glow showrooms

their eyes
watch children
with a wish came true desperation
reappearing as two toned stars
on the backs of generic milk cartons

yes
our eyes feel
all that they see

cello

locked inside a Moby playlist
heartbeats follow drumbeats

floods begin pelting rain resembling
your hair flowing through oiled hands

a weft and a weave mingling
through vanishing landscapes rekindling

ancient echoes vibrating through us
better than any drug prescribed you say

our bodies erupt across dented kitchen floors
barely contained until a phone call

sends silhouettes wading through memories
and once knowns become displaced words

as if seeing a moon rise
for the very first time

cello

we listen thru storm clouds resembling doubts
long left behind distances travelled a few days before

back to who knows where collapsing again
to hold a strangers hand and treat first responders

in a universe once created with inner smiles
we feel dulled in relapsing horrors

cello

from New Orleans to New York City
then back again seconds melt ice in a hot glass

an image of how slowly you undress
spatters like paint raging with thirst

being informed my driver takes cash only now
without asking to who knows where

cello

past impulses snagged dive deep within
a lack of controlling not to repeat gestures

hidden from ricochet protestors
we spy on conversations held down outside town halls

if this earth scars and floods too much more boss
we can bbq every damn weekend

cello

happiness begins with what is lost for words
without beginnings and endings

whispers reflect in charred pools
deranged second chances overflow

and the very same words wrap themselves around
outdated and deleted lightning struck live oaks

a faded yellow ribbon flapping in a wind
a sign acknowledging no safe passage guaranties

cello

under pillows you hide your beauty
reflected in your cup of decaffeinated coffee

unaffected by whatever stars have aligned
or designed to look forward to this knowing

a sense of redundant normality looms
as i roam moors and ever hungry cliffs

with postcard postage in time for Santa
hell bent on striking an oil soaked heaven

ignoring the uncapped markers dry on a table
where initials are carved with lost nails

cello

smoke signals our hands
battling everything impossible to stay clasped

the first time dancing reflecting the gypsy us
in a barn filled with shrieking ukuleles

clothed knowing any given moment
requires hijacking safe in trust watching how

you can weep yourself to sleep
before an august star explodes close by

and this taste of your laughter folds
reminiscent to reading your final text

we will make it out alive of this mess
with or without me muck boots

cello

another drizzle day passes in letters
started daze ago crumpled now ready to burn

stars shooting through heavenly moonbeams
recount stoned all night jaunts thru madhatten

you shedding your skins
with a smile hot as your ass

me a recycled envelope donning
crushed licked stamps

impossible to sleep typing notes
in a mystic spent misspelled youth

thunderstruck as sand castles rebuild
only to collapse around exploding variable options

until back beside the first carved moon
your eyes sparkle delight realizing

we are once again collapsible and universal
safely trapped inside a Moby playlist

quiet night shifts

Glow washes ketchup off dishes
in these quiet night shifts
her mind a bomb ticking reminder
trapped in timeless dungeons
noting with due efficiency
how lousy jobs rob treasures
found in whatever is thrown away

Glow dries chipped spinning plates
in these quiet night shifts
her mind a shell echoing poems
stuffed with holes equating to
cigarette breaks opening a pencil box
noting with due efficiency
craft pen ship is perfected after
sharpening wasted words

live bait

once
i watched you hide
in a glass reflecting
skeletons rattling hours
slipped on escapades
forgotten like fading scars
dangled on endless lines
determined to escape
overflowing ice buckets
laced in champagne and
tepid conversation

once
i watched you following
unknown footprints
on a path of burnt stars
visible in rising tides
sliced with moonlight
beside rock pool pockets
a sorceress conjuring
an ocean shimmering
with splinters

once
too numb to ask
flames cast in shadows
waited to be caught
in a dream catchers web
as your body tingling raw
whispered with wonder
hooked in laughter believing
we both cannot leave
this off book script
bound by endless tears

legend

word on camouflaged chimes street
echoes he is alive and kicking again

like a stubborn child bored with boo boos
and way too many gar gars

the frigid north fled backwards
receding into singed palmettos leaves

bundled up in this old medical office
after the cops left a mess raising cane

he rigged a shower outside
on a pallet with a hose

note to self

water moccasins dance in moonlight
under bare freezing feet

the ac and heat have yet to be fixed
freight trains continually rumble with toxins
keeping ghosts and debt collectors somewhat at bay
this is St Gabriel Louisiana after all

a mirror quasi laughs reinstating
he appears late again yet somehow feels early

memories ricochet through spanish moss
pens and brushes fire rounds of blanks
on bleached out sheets napkins and borrowed towels

far too many words to assemble a description of
how never enough light exudes ideas
illuminating truth

puddles reflect itching veins
laundry piles melt into cast off paintings

eyes scribble then collapse into 24/7 lists
without pain of time who really wants to exist

is anybody out there becomes a daily mantra
screeching with owls and local buzzards circling

fun amounts to placing quarters on well-worn tracks
the rummage of fingers dig deep into ashtray isles

if this curse requires a cure
blow burnt ash on tepid ink

unlit office rooms pacing reflections
on fingerprints and prescriptions

associated with this big hearted man
legend confirms he always carried a gun

one storm stroked night
he pulled all the stops on a sheriff trying
to stop him from delivering a baby

not too far from here
not that far from hope

some say legends are designed to keep fear at bay
sometimes legends reflect the unborn circling around us

sometimes legends occur at the oddest times of day
more often than not sipping coffee on a worn out stoop

beside rusting tracks embracing grace with gratitude
the legend of this place transforms magic into healing

tingling toxic

tingling toxic inside and out
café du monde coffee sipping

oblivious pink hearts
pulse over the veaux carre

on a crumbling royal street balcony
pigeon shit decorates broken screens

hidden from commerce
you sleep past sun burnt heat

deeper into a visual summation
treading over crushed beads

as glow in the dark bullets
see through glitter worn boots

with a need to return into our bodies
with an invasion of tongues

with soap in our shaken zombie hands
flushed from a rose scented bath

a couple of tabs delayed after
another coffee spilt returns

to slink through the crowd
like two reflections knowing

there is never enough time after destiny stains
their very own first time

shadow

when i cry you cry
when i speak you listen

what i see you see
what i feel you soothe

when cruel winds blow
you remain still

when rains drown
you stay dry

when suns shine
we both grow stronger

when bombs drop
you act calm

when i am old
your youth sustains

when crowds erupt
you join me

when i am lost
you remain near

when the deep within yells
you reply in silence

when zombie love exits
you return

unspoken land

unspoken land
rhymes parceled
breathing Palestine

sand dune waves roll
over bombed out paths
and forgotten royal carpets
surround barbed wire fences
chained to rusted coat hangers
dangling strange whispers

once an oasis of commerce
translates into a composition
war torn refugees refracted in
broken headlights mangled out of gas
on checkered tiled walls of mosques
shattered glass reflects
obliterated calm within
duct tape shadows

half bound speechlessness
waits in line as imagination
chews on death knocking
on streets brimming
with coffee and radios
tuned in to ignore
our precious promises
sparkling lack of conviction

burnt bunny ears

eleven of five am sparkles on
a scorched outpost of a waking day
a favorite time to be baked in silence
before the well spent ooze wears off

another heist completes progress
celebrated with beads hanging from trees
their branches glisten like sparklers
as the first stragglers all-night party people
wobble into our dungeon sanctuary
with arms and legs scratching bitten
raw lips smoked dry as delicate butterflies
pinned to crumbling cemetery walls

before saying whatz your name backwards
rouge eyes stare at my lit cigarette
and a bunny suit appears nestling beside me
fag burns and tears on the tops of her ears
reflect smudged eye shadow and fresh bruises

closer than cuddles she reaches for my pack
straight off the bat asking what do i do for a living
beside looking like i need to do something else
like ordering a double glazed in possibilities

canny laughter often suggests a monkey
laughing on backs uncannily laughing
and before tattooed money is exchanged
from deep within my pocket of holes
finite feels grateful and thanks the bartender
for acknowledging all the mistakes
years have outweighed logic

meanwhile bunny suit with burn marks
passes out on my buckled shoulder
before ever finishing her bummed cigarette
i exit my family of circus freaks
and return to a cage mirrored without
regrets buried unreachable

mobile home

torn
fishing boats
smash against levees
like bare toes stubbed
against concrete bed posts
broken bottles reflect abstractions
through the pine needle floor where
lean to caravans with juke joint rhythm ghosts
burst spontaneously onto refugees cursing closed
bars and casinos imagining themselves all beating creation
tortured now in limbo moments swiftly silenced within
storms lingering on evolutions doorstep and pinned
to this marsh sodden woodland makeshift campsite
where washed out words trapped inside ink
fade like a note written resembling your
delicate illegible scrawl reading there
is plenty of time to thirst for
innocence after you quit
navel gazing and figure
out how to turn
my ruins on
again

you ask me

you
ask me
would it be
grand if my behavior
added up evenly and equally
to the sum of all your
visibly stagnant parts
every time my truck brakes fail
or this bully stained banker
refuses my check

you
ask me
is it oh so fine
when i grace a smile
you smile back as we sit
zoned slouching in silence
attempting to ignore
rowdy local strangers
wafting dope smitten
fizzy flavored gin
obviously having
way more fun
than either of our
sun burnt asses

you
ask me
would it be oafish
if we blame pesky
hot spots on the sun
for the countless times
i slip thru ever widening cracks
devoured on visions desire

tangled thread bare sheets
sleeping continents apart
strangled in caged love
and self imposed strife
as you text if it is okay
to once in a while
walk off my screen porch
and never ever look out
over your shoulder

you ask me
is this bliss to release
anger instead of fear
coming home uptight
freaked out and morphed in
because you were forced to smile
and kiss your lily white
bosses fat ass

you ask me
are we way too
hip to quote as a joke
in this grandiose tasteless
fingerpicking excuse of a town
jean genet claiming chivalry
to every one horse trader
all believing hell often happens
here on razor fenced earth
and to enter any kind of
heaven almighty
never cost no
two nickels
and a dime

you ask me
if hilarious equals
hysterically believing
every fake news feed
seen on the bewitching tube
made for better neighbors
too funny to wake and realize
after all this meditation and exercise
after every ladder climbed
imagination leads us back
to those sacred places
where all of us
once belonged

overpass

under the overpass
lacy folds away her deck chair and
torn pages salvaged from discarded whispers
foraged in one more forgotten yesterday
depicting half-baked daydreams floating
endless in a sea of unshaven worldz
driven in paths of obscure circles
her secret hopes now visualize
the over mortgaged home
finally going up in flames

under the overpass
mickey unwraps his pipe cleaning art
once known locally at many a craft fair
he finishes every conversation
before any audible word becomes
a wee tad buttered or confused
before screeching demons forever
blister the voices regrets summon

under this overpass
squelched with footprints
collaged in worlds of misspelt menus
meaningless questions boil into
cave like suggestions mimicking martha
congealing with reminiscences
her deep pockets now laced with holes
and half sentences melt in a sun singing
outdated poems etched to no one

under the overpass
a sight for sore eyes wobbles
with mirrored wonky shades cracked
on the nose of carlos dissecting shadows into

laughter long gone like the daze of his youth
rattled in scriptures and words translating
themselves now into cheap blow jobs
safe knowing his number is scratched
on endless bathroom
mirrors and stalls

under this overpass
life huddles with ticks and lice
safe in sewers of who cares quicksand
knowing these uncaring times
keeps the traffic flowing

washed out parade

your belt buckle broke about an hour ago
holding foraged designer ripped jeans
we stagger as wayward shadows through pockets
of unlit streets drenched in rising flood water

storm flies mist the air in this borrowed room
damp towels disclose escaping desire abandoned
like canvases shot through with bullet holes
ripped apart yet open to confuse our
madness to rejoin the last of many
washed out parades

rain beating rain hammers on tin
rooftops and empty dime stores
abandoned cars burnt out past recognition
park permanently lodged beside
rows of shot gun houses
long ago forgotten

buckets of stones ricochet with gunshots
thrown from a crazed giant or our undisclosed
roommate blurting this ice age creeps
sloughed and predicable like a cat
following a wounded bird or our masks
cut up like words buried and unreachable

knowing our hearts beat nerves
and spinal cords yearn to break free
from lack of control and the betrayal
of muffled familiars bruised into
screams and errors risen
with oil stained puddles lacking
any kind of form or commitment armed
with pots brewing nuclear organic tea

backwards feels familiar again
before falling forward towards
echoes rekindled in vagrancies
time wasted mimics

grocery list

can this poem reach out to save a life
can broken verse make for a healthier place

for example what if i list food companies
using toxic Monsanto chemicals

does writing such a tome
represent quasi radical

either way here is a grocery list
before cows become castles

before another pig eats its own brains
before another child is poisoned for profit

—note to reader
this list is rather mundane
unfit for any refrigerator
be aware if rhythms are apathetically corny
it is a cheap trick learned in high school—

so here we have Aunt Jemima and Quaker
Betty Crocker and Bisquick mixed in with General Mills and
Duncan Hines

Jiffy and Ms Butterworths mold with Pepperidge Farms and
Campbells Post Cereals blend in with Phillip Morris tobacco
who now own Kraft Foods
go figure

Hershey's Nestle is selling soiled water with Carnation and
Holsum Interstate Bakeries stir fried with Best Foods and Knorr

Nabisco and Nature Valley are alongside Kelloggs and Pillsbury
Heinz and Hellmans chasing with Hunts

KC Masterpiece joins Frito-Lay and Pepsi,
Delicious Brand Cookies swirls with Famous Amos Keebler/
Flowers Industries

Banquet and Green Giant Somehow join Healthy Choice
ConAgra and Kid Cuisine Are laced with Stouffers Lean Cuisine

Marie Callenders runs with Smart Ones and Power Bar Brands
Chef Boyardee and Hormel Loma Linda and Morning Star blend
with Lipton Unilever

Uncle Ben's Rice-a-roni Pasta-roni Tombstone Pizza and Totinos
Contain the same amount of poison as Pringles and Pop Secret.

Orville Redenbacher Proctar and Gamble
Work well together with V-8 Coca Cola and Cool-aid

Minute Maid Cadbury/Schweppes throw up the rear
All mixed together with Prego Pasta and Ragu sauce

leaving me with little else to say
except we are what we eat
and have a Wonder Bread day

anyplace special

letz plan a trip
you and me
before us is old
before time turns cold
we can exit untamed
without a name
or take a train in flames
beside sea shore smiles
bathed making memories
sweet as scented wine
we can crumble on cliffs
below sand castles melting
like staircases laced
in delicate bluebells
lost as forgotten hours
shatter the worn
before returning home
riding the last bus
before safe as snails
on the torn back seat
draw another map
wondering perhaps
someone someday
might ask a friend
to plan a trip following
our very own
anyplace special

under a burning buffalo blanket

under a burning buffalo blanket
we shroud knowing this flint blade
this carcass dried out covering
protects native infants from slaughter
as love consumes bullets outweighing guns
stolen below sea level with whispers
wailing to conform inside this vintage VW bus
scorched with pretense no future forgave
these tribes fused in pipelines scattering
flesh eating bones and spider web dwellings

under a burning buffalo blanket
firefighters volunteers and medics
work beyond imaginations bled out beliefs
while back stage suited guys snicker
our water is copyrightable

under a burning buffalo blanket
i miss your voice beyond this storm
forgiven as desire moves inward alive
a mirage floating towards falling burnt leaves
rekindled in scorched flight perhaps
strong enough to watch our own backs
as another cluster fuck grins amen

picnic

a picnic longing this april may day
a plastic igloo open mouthed waiting

minutes climb over themselves
fire ants spell out your name like a rash

nervous hands rarely are much fun
unless they are mine lost in your hair

the drum of city traffic feels extinctive
impatient pigeons fight over salt and vinegar crisps

a bug bite soon becomes a scratch
a red mark unleashing an itch in ruins

we sit cocooned with forgetfulness
half naked bursting in baked laughter

zombies pace around us
their sentence an endless watch of frowns

raindrop

oh to be a raindrop
falling on silk

to hear your heartbeat
so close and yet

seconds speed away
on a journey undefined

thunder reflects
fires burnt in our eyes

demons on the half shell

long ago in the past few seconds
when sweet nothings shot through our veins
the shells we hide in crippled with cures
kept us safe behind this vacant parking lot
both in one body
then us

sometime ago in the past last relapse
Joan Jett re rendered Crimson and Clover
a smoking grill laced with garlic and lemon exhaled
before abstract thoughts scattered
over a windy Chimes Street onto concrete steps
laced with mysterious and new
temptations echoed
wrapped in one body
then us

not so long ago chasing a riddle called love
vague clarity sent our salted crackers tasting
like silver spoons melting on your breath
laying in a heap in your bathroom
i swore i would kill you if you ever died again
blind in one body
then us

climbing awkward yet charged
oh so long ago across this levee crisscrossed
by a thunder sky river ripples eclipse
and cosmic pillars of the universe
dance heaven bound as our slugging heartbeats
overdose with fingers twitching
burnt in one body
then us

long ago on the same day
this time bound around
scars of life mirror sweet nothings
yet compared to the stains of deception
wrapped around these flashing cop lights
an inward standstill meshed backwards claims
i will take a bullet for both of us
stung in one body
then us

long ago kinda like today
demons dance on the half shell
and like it or not we continue to drink
from the same spilled cup
toe tapping to Lonesome Sundown
under the sweltering shade of swaying banana leaves
laced in one body before returning
once again to us

broken hymns

broken hymns
snap chords of humility
remembered as silver ushered along
speechless dusty aisles
held together in sticky pews
withered with voices defining
my childhood sins
naturally hell
bent

broken hymns
are anthems for children
taught how to behold the unseen
and let go of reality
broken hymns
gate crashed my day dreams
filled with uncharted places
far away from these tired exchanges
laced in a childlike realization
i will never truly know who
my father really is

take off

as always at airports
or other points of departure
silent confusion mingles with impulses
instinct making survivors stronger

questions appear as quotations
and for many asking if the god we trust in pain
differs from the gods we seek in pleasure
no cure offered seems to stop the shaking
white knuckled emotions
a lack of control

as always at airports
or other points of departure
i recognize how so many beautiful masks
remain perfect strangers
take today for a hindered fact
frozen windows reflect baggage handlers
appearing fragile potential victims perhaps
working to protect dreams from escaping
one bombed out scenario to another
unable to laugh at random pointlessness
as if saving what they know until later
somehow makes a difference

as always at airports
or other points of departure
in the blindness of pleasure just before take off
memories add to burdens stabbing
silent fears with knives and forks poking
an invisible inevitable bubble
often called hope to see you soon

the bewilderment of dreams

not to wallow in ashes
a future reborn sings louder than words
not to sing in distances of bayous reclaimed
perhaps too much get to and not enough give to
a chained mask crackles and past portraits swoon
yet these words get to sit here humbled
beside a king fisherman and his desk
Huey P Long no less
and yes i get to take the tour
and yes i get to wash my hands
in a clean sink

Cicadas say
listen one Woody Guthrie night
alone and surrounded by you who
continually bombard a way to life
you who question the resources of this life
be mindful executed standards
equal diddle de squat to a typewriter
lived in a mirage of accomplishments
greater than anything this jester imagines
nestled in visions glory of imagination
i sway to the bewilderment of dreams

Cicadas repeat
and in the gift to read with live sleepless
our chorus bathes at a river edge
raged in moonlight and armed in laughter
yellow skies glow brighter tonight with
a belly full of moons eclipsing
no shade for the wicked

Cicadas follow
red stick downtown
this punk on a mission consumes
borrowed pen and paper before
last rites turn over leaves

Persimmon
to know the weight of bullets
before ever pulling the trigger

pelicans protect our bathed uncertainty
no flags in sight we enter stunned
to promises bamboo makes lucky duck stands
with freezing drizzle on our eyelids

a search for squirrel and rabbit
demented as these wild boars
fishing till our fingers bleed awake
extinguished in chicory and coffee
on country roads destinations
24/7 grits at louis café

an end game reward
finding a treasure trove of mushrooms
mid december you may well recall
to dance giddy all night bouncing
with the bayou on chimes street
before wallowing again at a rivers calm
in sunshine yellow grows brighter with industry
yet this punk on a mission
consumes to beg borrow and steal
to create the next line unwritten

comet movements commitments to practice
inside the bewilderment of dreams

confederate jasmine umbrellas unfold
perfumed on dragonfly wings

strange echoes reflect mirrors of bygone
reflections deleted into quotations

those damn eagles are eating all me walnuts
they are squirrels my lord and local pecans

i always pay the ferryman an extra dime you fiend
we double back on ice cubes around here

where ripples mimic bayous seen in a glow
across this ocean of a river

mighty commerce communes with his or her
or better still unites all in a journey

sliced in a swamp scape back drop
a visual exit to mankind brews

to wish nothing less channeled smoking outside
stolen by memories and remembered names

accepted to be merry on passover
yet swaddled in gypsy blood

to work volunteer lsu traffic cop duty
loaded directing ole miss fly off their rockers

to save every dime to be merry at pinettas
to sip on a cold beer in the laplace store six am sharp

to honor bloody toes lost slicing
this frozen cane we chew on

to fall from grace backwards into heavens
consumed with history on the rebound

to whisper persimmon in your ear
before tonight devours

and yes there is a song
many in fact yet to be sung
and yes this is a song sung before
and yes there are places
to heal time and space
and yes this place echoes
preserve louisiana
preserve louisiana

craving

we might need
more than words tonight
to pull out from underneath
the exhumed rage you consumed
and i doubt a tub of ice cream
glued together with jelly beans
is going to cut the cake

we might need
more than an unforgiving
tropical storm beating against
my trucks windshield to remind you
what you have been searching for
half your damned waking life
walked out less than
an hour ago

we might need
something more than a few
dollars in the electric meter
to find a light to find your keys
and repair the front door lock
and make damn well sure
your ex stays away
for real this time

clock on the wall

clock on the wall quit your truth
give me something new to chew on

help me not believe how stung undone
life often sounds like ringing ears

or three stubby ringed fingers
stuffed down my throat

equals two of them
never minds

grant me instead clock on the wall
true mysterious of time filled with extremes

laced in waking dreams and unwept secrets
lost in hours deciphering how can i free

the gnawing whimpering dogs
chained and beaten in blistering cages

next
door

tommie boy

tommie boy hobbles
through thinly sliced masked worlds

a faceless cough
housed in a coughing crowd

raised believing in fear
enmeshed him to a sewer

cleaning crappy bathroom stalls
laced with cockroach shit and cum

tommie boy wobbles
to scrub puke off sticker walls

in a past life some can assume
he might have been a hero

a one string guitarist
masquerading in a traveling circus

tommy boy shivers
thanks to his medication

as the crowd gaily parties over
his buckled bloody feet

oh tommy boy
our sweet heart tommy boy

buy this lost soul
something strong to drink

oh yes raise a glass
and sing along

with tommy boy
our sweet heart tommy boy

you know we all love him
our tommy boy our tommy boy

kicking a can in madhatten

easy to dismiss this lock down
six flights up boiled success feels humbled
by ongoing storms plagued in spinning plate worlds

bulls grab their own horns as masked mankind
sways inward towards one room tombs
and unknown killers fill the air

you enter electrified
immaculately dressed exploding in venezuela swagger
after a complicated day unaffected by booze

engaged over olives and wine
the visible lack of furniture confuses your entourage
soon dismissed you confess inheritances boil souls

in a city where souls lose time you say my work can
be nailed and duct taped to crumbling subways
until they bleed out dry

adieu with shaking hands money is exchanged
we part loaded in laughter
no sign or discourse until several years later

zealous swaggers recognize as like attracts like
the same lack of furniture confusing
the same confused entourage

how is your soul kicking a can in madhatten
you ask again have you not heard
i opened a gallery beside tomkins park

stop in anytime with some new work
and blow their brains out before
my next group show

soup kitchen song

lord
oh dear lord
hear me prayers

pull me upward
as time descends
into your scared crib

grind these bones
into a delicate paste
dish out my blood
on used paper plates

lord
oh dear lord
hear me prayers

take all of me
without a trace
create new thoughts
to relieve all hope
served in these lines
with sausage gumbo
and steaming rice

lord
oh dear lord
hear me prayers

suck me dry
into your holy realm
let cockroaches fight over
my shriveled brain

give gratitude a hug
as brawling alley cats
lick clean my
contaminated
remains

hunkering down

one whispers to two
are you awake my angel

two whispers to one
no fall asleep will you

one caresses two
my hands are yours

two touches one
yes you are dreaming

born again

oh to be
born again she
yawns after finding
her glasses then a blunt pen
pushes him back over before proceeding
to scrape through today having spent
dimes on a six pack of stella highlife
often resembles disfigured enlargements
she continues spiraling past any chance
to reconnect marks captured on
bloody concrete curbs being
constantly told upwards and
onwards is the only way to go
and yet backwards becomes a
path naturally filled with holes
until someday we reach new
sensations resembling falling from
rooftops where religion and greed
caves into every women given
the right to own her
own set of balls

blank pages

in disorder for order
to scratch or carve out
a whole one minute line
an impression lingers
throughout this evening
alone and yelling all you wanted
withdrew into unnamed stars and stripes
eclipsed with a moon and hounded by
memories accustomed to cheesy endings
covered now in moldy note books

one blank page reads less likely
is the best bet to bet on
hidden minutes collapse
into hour long rivers
dissolving sleepless shadows
punctuated with progressive regress
as questions answering who reads words
spills every time coffee scolds
and the rejection slip arrives
wrapped or unwrapped
disfigured or torn
an overstatement of the obvious
bathed tonight as you bathe
beside this haunted bayou
this soul quenching home
shimmering with snakes

suburban circles

one two three
another boundary four
1976 ends a business brunch
with a strip tease menu
finery topped off
on a nice creamed sundae

five to six
the longest minutes past seven
absent fathers dare tell their wives
the finance gods have lost it all
and bankrupted heaven
leaving behind unhitched up skirts
the fantasy p.a.
ms supreme suspenders
throwing a brick into brixton

late again at ten to nine
lonely housewives click on tv
the remote control to escape
and fade into soapy lifestyles
prozac on hand
all in the name of losing a pound
before the husband plunders in
eleven or twelve

then back to one
beamer screeching
retirement handshakes
relocate again
someplace sunny perhaps
pack off the brats
first class of course
resume marmalade parties

refined sugar tastes sweet
unlike their lost son
who slammed the front door
screaming as he tripped
slap bang on his face

your doggy done a whoopy
better change the lawn
or something

clean to the bone

draw nearer into the light
not so shy anymore

singe fragile textured wings
marooned on endless isles in fires

where fake news rattles with laughter
and destiny unbuckles rekindled and fearless

on this our makeshift raft
abstract in believing squeezed moments

found holding treasures sliding
in and out of waking dreams

buck shot scars outwit inner wounds
embracing new beginnings

love gnaws
clean to the bone

text

is there
a line or two
i can text you boo
wandering in a lifetime
perplexed by capsules
citations and infringements
with dizzy thoughts echoed
through a maze complicated by
natural instinct and short changed
dreams buried in baked rusty corners
searching for a common ground
to understand each other
for loving so much yet
unable to accept
ourselves for
being oh so
different

what if

what if all
this spinning faded
and the teeth clawing
inside our melted minds
burst into a purring
tabby cat asleep
on your naked lap
and this icy north
wind turned south
to blow warm air over
the nape of our necks
and trickles of tickling sweat
ran down your inner thigh
underneath a printed
leopard gown cloaked
in our own ruin knowing
zombie love has no clue how
anything unfamiliar becomes
a truth filling the hour glass
with how shall we meet again
past ongoing disasters
and sullen domestic fears
back to where two
busted hearts
bleed as one

sirens replace mad song birds

sirens replace
mad song birds
blunt pencils scattered
on a desk migrate into
bullets ever hungry to be
wasted with no damage
control in sight thoughts become
blurry reminder eggs over easy
facts cracking in a low grade culture
concealing points of departure plans
to jump off a soggy trailer sinking
in a swamp or an overloaded merry
go round lacking any form of merry
in response to another ice cap melting
forest fires raging pandemics breathing
opinionated solutions hump themselves
to sleep in an abused overly trodden
world exchanging love for fear
in the spectacle of democracies
commercial smiles resembling
outdated ring tones and
newfangled masks

and yet
for all of the above
for some odd reason
this pandemic grip feels
far more productive than
fake news prattling on
debating how politicians
can fix problems if our
actions cease fire

and common decency
dissolves into puddles
reflecting apathy
hunkering down

one whispers to two
are you awake angel

two whispers to one
no fall asleep will you

one caresses two
hands rejoin hands

two touches one
day dreaming alive

life aches

life aches
to begin again
new born bulbs
answer with an urgency
gnawing like mothers sore
nipples bleeding in make
shift cribs of teething infants
swaddled in stained sheets
between pockets and skin
fixed stars explode leaving trace
fragments of lipstick memories
or spent hopes laced in
used masks and gloves
as birds pecking
at frozen puddles in
a worn wolf moon light
fall helpless beside buildings
boarded up to become mere
scratch offs with musty curtains
flapping signals across abandoned
rows of confessions scrawled on torn
paper one reads if you let dreams
sleep your life will rot away into
stolen hours with spoken interludes
and mushy clouds lingering on hotel
ceilings and scratched shoulders as
broken night slips between bruised
thighs before daylight displays a
reluctance to appear on chiselled
streets with dew damp footprints
melting into lost regrets and
burnt out eyes ensconced on
on this double decker bus
late for work knowing

there is no chance
life aches to
begin again
on this double decker bus
late for work knowing
there is no chance
life aches to
begin again

take off

as always at airports
or other points of departure
silent confusion mingles with impulses
and instinct makes the survivor stronger

questions appear as quotations
and for many asking if the god we trust in pain
differs from the gods we seek in pleasure
no cure offered seems to stop the shaking
white knuckled emotions
losing control

as always at airports
or other points of departure
i recognize how so many beautiful masks
remain strangers to me
take today for a hindered fact
frozen windows the baggage handlers
appear fragile
potential victims perhaps
protecting our dreams
from escaping one criminal
scenery to another
unable to laugh at
the random pointlessness
of it all
as if saving what we know
until later might somehow
make a difference

as always
at airports
or other points of departure
in the blindness of pleasure

just before take off
memories can add
to the burden stabbing
silent fears with knives
or forks poking the invisible
inevitable bubble
often called

us

within time

the stage blurs opaque
built on misplaced truth

an abandoned parking lot
mulled by flowering weeds

busting through widening cracks
photo shopped into back drops

and ornamental proliferations
defy this dismal silence

on this our first day
outside time

photos stapled to soggy walls
flap on wet spray paint silhouettes

moments ago you tagged

few fade
into the dust
we trust

there is little question
our laughter is contagious

our bodies liquid spillage
glued without wanting
anyone else to infect

as backstage echoes
whimper in wrinkled wombs

and shards of chipped paint dance
peeled through buckled curtains

a damaged world reflecting
distorted mirror views

in this our last time
within time

lightning sparks glisten
calculated stage fright

alongside fallen props resembling
cartoon cardboard cities

burnt leaves
open wounds

cast images and abandoned scars
trace memories across your skin

huddled together fragile
without dice we gamble on fireflies

cupped in whispering hands
trembling as chaos slips through

on this our first day
without time

eaten alive

stained in last minutes
the remnants of new beginnings
follow 500 miles far less travelled
to this rusty lone star restaurant
where paper napkins share
the same sad waiters
lack of joy

finally you say i bet
you would lick all my leftovers
from this filthy plate if i exited
towards that disgusting bathroom
and gave you second chance
number two hundred
and six

i nod mumbling
cold mixed greens
stuck between stained teeth
sweet cheeks i promise to eat
nothing else except you alive
side tracked noticing through
the smeared windows passing
trucks and mini vans sloshing by
with prayers and pop tunes
intermingling in heavy
over easy diesel air

i hope you are
going to floss tonight
for sure trying to figure out

what circle of hell they have
descended into sighing over
twangs repenting above below
and through us all how do people
exactly live here you cringe handing
me a soggy bill before shouting in the
direction of a kitchen hole in a wall
what makes tasteless fried fat
so damn fuckin
expensive

bail out

finally
enough cash to get
the front end realigned
between trumpet bloomers
and busted sand bags of memories
failed as actions recede into hunkering down
through another storm with what is the point
of packing your mothers soggy thesaurus
when we have limited drinking water
and stray dogs to feed along miles
of out of gas freeways divided in
both directions by concrete
barriers collecting fatalistic
miles of trash where
emergency hard hats replace
waves of football team spirit
baseball caps and parking lots
now morphing into tented housing
complexes for the unmanned
unnamed mobile dead wobbling
on snickers to escape a vice grip
clutched in hands resembling cell phones
famished of width band vocabularies
and worn washed out words
once known for their
common decency

dip closer

indeed this could be our longest first time
watching milk on a makeshift stove scold

without so much as a care for icicle tears
inside this campervan home we imagine

safe knowing our needs continue to crawl
under pebbles softened with salt

we dip closer into molten moons
laced in trances and countless lost hours

passing foreclosure signs stapled to fence posts
or slapped on shopfront windows as frozen words

men bark with their dogs at children dancing in rags
rain soaked grime watching their blistered feet swell

you say if i could only believe in honest confession
before scribbling inwardly i want to cling film you again

before the ratchet shadows of time
whip us back into some sort of new shape

beg to differ

beg to differ
lie if you have to

to tell the truth
try to undo

daily routines
plaguing existence

the cat has been fed
the dog is asleep

a blistering winter awaits
with no place safe to go

yes

beg to differ
lie if you have to

as long as there are
a few frozen words

to scribble
and chew on

we might make it down river
and sleep with who ever

before routine returns
and words end up

repeating themselves
on a tell-tale spin

as we find ourselves
once again alone

with no place
safe to go

body parts

we are all here again
inside the same cave asking
why bother adore our outer and
inner self with the growing knowledge
passages curated through time are no longer
negotiable cures in order to survive

regardless of how
the gun is loaded
regardless of who
pulls the trigger

we are all here again
random body parts stuck
together with stitched up wounds
puppet like unable to accept there are
two sides to every man women and child
one side named good and the other
some call evil yet we no longer ask
where do these two sides meet

regardless of how
the gun is loaded
regardless of who

pulled the trigger

one word at a time

to begin to end with words
some given many taken back

a universe exploding
a craving to create

encouraged by life
translated into mystery

published
or yet to be written

to begin to end with words
glistening as stars glisten

blankets of unknowns sparkle
transformed into galactic tapestries

to begin to end with words
restless to escape voids

blistered fingers and thumbs
hide in the shadows

before magically reappearing
by hook or by crook

similar to a hunter perhaps
alone in these frozen woods

a loaded shot gun impatiently waiting
for the next meal to arrive

to push through fear
the doubt and useless guilt

regardless of how many words
already appear perfect

in their organic composition
their unbiased truth

before aiming
before pulling trigger

regardless of unpaid bills
piled on the dashboard

regardless a gas gauge
flickering on empty

as you drive to the store
with a pocket full of loose change

gathered from mason jars
for another pack of smokes

for another six pack of beer
before circumstances out way morals

going deeper within
the emptiness of tonight

melts into daybreak
as a thin grey slice of dawn

translates a world into a word
then two maybe three

before the first birds sing
and a sentence is completed

helpless and vulnerable
fresh stains on blank pages

one word at a time